AMITY
peace poems

AMITY
peace poems

Editor
Sahana Ahmed

NEW DELHI CALCUTTA

Hawakal
PUBLISHERS

HAWAKAL PUBLISHERS
70 B/9 Amritpuri, East of Kailash, New Delhi 65
33/1/2 K B Sarani, Mall Road, Calcutta 80

Email info@hawakal.com
Website www.hawakal.com

Cover designed by Bitan Chakraborty

First edition (paperback) December 2022

ISBN: 978-93-91431-84-6 (paperback)

Price: INR 400 | USD 16.99

for
Runu *and* Haider

M E S S A G E

I am glad that Sahana Ahmed, India Country Chair - World Peace with G100, has edited an anthology of peace poems 'Amity'.

Featuring 47 writers from 8 countries, the book is a soulful tribute to efforts of peace in all forms.

I wish the publication all success.

(NAVEEN PATNAIK)

Phone : | Office : 0674-2531100, 2531500, 2535100 (Fax)
| Residence : 0674-2591099, 2590299, 2590833 (Fax)
e-mail : cmo@nic.in I twitter : twitter.com/CMO_Odisha I Facebook : facebook.com/CMO.Odisha

INTRODUCTION

This book contains ninety-five poems by forty-seven writers from France, India, Israel, Japan, the Netherlands, the Philippines, the United Kingdom, and the United States of America. Sixty-two poems cover the five interrelated and interdependent spheres of peace, as described by the National Peace Academy, USA: the personal, the social, the political, the institutional, and the ecological. Sixteen poems are about the absence of peace, seventeen poems make a plea for it. These poems are listed in the alphabetical order of the contributors' family names.

The idea for this anthology was born out of the confluence of two of my roles: a poet and India Country Chair—World Peace at G100. G100 is a group of global women leaders that comprises a league of luminaries, including Nobel laureates, heads of state, entrepreneurs, and philanthropists. Twenty-two of the featured writers have an affiliation to G100 or connected platforms, such as ALL Ladies League and Women's Indian Chamber of Commerce and Industry. Two poets are members of The Denim Club, He-for-She champions in support of the G100 Vision Statement: To create an equal, progressive, and inclusive environment for women worldwide.

My own vision for this collection was simple. I was interested in honest writing; all types of poetry, from free verse to traditional forms, were welcome. It was crucial to me that voices from different quarters were heard regardless of previous writing experience. So, we have *soi-disant* closet poets rubbing shoulders with those who have earned international acclaim; more than a dozen *Amity* contributors have at least one literary honour to their credit.

There are many ways to make the world a peaceable place. You can listen with an open mind. You can visit a museum. You can reduce your carbon footprint. You can learn another language. You can donate to charity. You can walk your neighbour's dog. You can draw and paint. You can read more books.

I hope you enjoy this one.

SAHANA AHMED
December 2022

Koi jape Rahim Rahim, koi jape hai Ram
Das Kabir hai prem pujari, dono ko parnaam

~ Kabir Das

[One recites Rahim; one chants Ram
Kabir salutes both and worships love.]

CONTENTS

VINITA AGRAWAL
Writers Without Borders

Rain waters listen to secret flowers beneath the soil
The night settles to darken the bottoms of trees
My ink flows, mingles without geography.

Every tear fills the jar of the waiting moon
And despite the hell-towers all around
Writers resurrect the doors of broken thoughts.

Every star branch trickles with blood's bitterness
War reigns across borders, land fights land
Religion versus religion. Everywhere, a divided stand.

Yet, my fellow pen, fellow nib, fellow hand
Though the needle of pain pierces your darkened veins
Write! So that man may understand man.

Write sans borders, fences, frontiers
Make thick the river of sentiments
Call swiftly for peace, for love.

History doesn't change that fast
Time doesn't bend easily
Change doesn't happen overnight.

Still, the votives of clattering flowers
Fall gentler on the chest of pebbles
The sun comes out again...because of words of dissent.

Tremors of joy run through your fingers
As darkness builds a dawn
Write on!

For countries war torn,
Let darkness build a dawn
Wherever you are...Write on.

Previously published in *Gallerie Magazine* (ed. Bina Sarkar, June 2017)

Epitaph On A Laburnum Tree

A Laburnum by the school parapet
where bodies were butchered, where lives were shred.

Now I stammer when the sun shines its light.
I reek of blood by the howl of the night.

Yellow no more, I am blisters of red.
Red leaves, red branches, ghosts of red, red, red.

I grow no more–I cry to the pale winds.
I shall stay this way, for by hate I'm singed.

I weep over scarred and bulleted walls
like broken mothers who wept, cried, and called.

Tender names of beloved tender babes.
Caressed and buried in two-by-three graves.

The bullets–they made smithereens of hearts.
Tore lives into excruciating parts.

A Laburnum by the school parapet
where bodies were butchered, where lives were shred.

One Half

One half prayed to Allah, the other to Ram, my friend
Such was the line slashing broken hearts, my friend

Unfettered were tears, birds, leaves, winds
Horizons were fettered and barbed, my friend

Grandparents moaned like suffering animals
When skies choked on clouds of death, my friend

A single language wobbled in voices two
Razor tongues plunged in saffron and green, my friend

Old cultures slumped on a new history
White dove of time bloodied and butchered, my friend

Even to look that way is taboo now
Such was the severing from that old love, my friend

Tonight, a tender breeze wraps me in scents
I'm on my knees, open your door, my friend

Sahana Ahmed
Fashionable In France

I love it here. Rue de This, Rue de That, Art Deco
unlimited. But they let their dogs poop everywhere.

My shoes were Aldo. Ruined now. *"Merde!"*

A voice protests. Not a dog mom; just some
neighbourhood nag yelling French things at me.

She is too fast, too loud, my Google français inutile.

What's wrong, is my face too Delhi?

Dress = Zara
Jacket = Mango
Bag = LV
My fashion's on point for *ze* woman, I think.

I let her get closer, I let her see my iPhone.
She has one of her own.

I sigh, adjust my hijab, and take off my shoes.

merde: French for "shit"
ze: eye dialect for "the"
Previously published in *101 Words* (June 28, 2019)

Dear Sister

Beyond
the ways of my sun,
the germs in my veins,
the brass in my claims,
my *purdah*, my mane—
I am you too.

The wounds of my walls,
the tombs of my lanes,
the thrones of my queens,
my *mehfils*, my rains—
are your home too.

Thursdays of fire,
Fridays of steel,
yearnings of *yakshas*
and foreskins of *djinns*
are your shame too.

Remember,
when we meet next,
look me in the eye,
ask me—
            Who bore you?

And I will unstitch my heart
and show you new ways
to etch your mother's name.

purdah: the practice in certain Muslim and Hindu societies of screening
women from men or strangers, especially by means of a curtain
mehfil: Urdu for "gathering"
yaksha: Sanskrit for "nature-spirit"
djinn: Arabic for "spirit" or "demon"

Previously published in *The Woman Inc.* (May 2020)

A Beginner's Guide To Indian Gods For The Wannabe Hippie

a is for allah—beneficent, kind
b is for buddha, wisdom defined

christ, on a mission, patient with time
durga, harbinger of parties divine

elephant-ganesha, clearer of paths
fire-lord agni, wrapped up in wrath

ganga, the giver, eternally pure
hanuman, the mighty, courier of cure

indra, of heavens, thunder and storm
jagannath, the wide-eyed, simple of form

krishna, the prankster, lover-in-chief
lakshmi, of bounties beyond belief

mahavir= ahimsa, empty of hate
nataraja, the dancer, greatest of great

(ik) onkar: one god, one with no second
parvati, of massifs, gentle and fecund

queen bhuvaneshwari, universal diva
rama, the main man, champion of shiva

sharada/saraswati, lady of letters
tara, the tantric, demon-baiter

ushas, the gleaming dawn of all breaths
vishnu, the hero, preventer of deaths

w is for waruna, liege of the seas
x is the god(dess) inside you and me

yama, the undead, judge of our lives
zoroaster—prophet we need to revive

Previously published in *Madras Courier* (October 29, 2022)

MOUMITA ALAM
We Are At Peace
They make a desolation and call it peace.
~ Agha Shahid Ali

i
In a government-run school
the recess bell rings.
A mad rush to the dining room.
White eyes are on the plates.
It's an egg day in the mid-day meal calendar.

ii
In the valley,
the khakis are frisking for dissent
from breasts to toenails.
Do they search their hearts too?

iii
At 7.30:
She was beaten almost to death.

At 9:
Her husband is salivating at the
the smell of the delicious mutton curry

she is cooking.
Today he is extra hungry.

We share our bed with predators
and call it peace.

iv
She was raped by her cousin.
How many times
she lost count/
Abba Jaan discovered
the all-healing panacea—Marriage.
Ammi nodded her head.

The cousin was looking like a prince charming
in the groom's dress.
Only the clarinets failed to blow in tune.

PRIYA ANAND
A Message To The Almighty

My prayers glide on air currents
They travel to distant lands
They bow to the many Gods
that have made their homes there
They dip and swoop and surf the wind
The words whirl and dance
The letters drop one by one or all at once
They find a kindred soul in other words
and form new sentences in unknown lyrical languages
They may sound strange and exotic
but the essence is the same
A message to the Almighty

A Postcard From Hikkim

A postcard from the highest post office in the world
makes its way home to Bangalore.
I choose one which features the post office,
indistinguishable from the other homes in the village
except for the Red India Post sign that adorns it.
Penned on the card are a few words
written by hands unfamiliar with a pen,
A forgotten skill tested again.
Rs. 50 for international and
Rs. 10 within India is the amount.
Let's write a few more, I think
but the mind and hand falter.
The postcard with its fellow compatriots
lies supine in an old brown sack
that has made this journey several times.
Hikkim to Kaza and then to Manali
on an old Himachali bus that zigzags its way
across treacherous mountainous terrains,
avoiding falling boulders and a rock-strewn road,
a bumpy journey across Spiti.
The card shakes and rolls
in rhythm with the bus wheels.
It doesn't peek out to seek

the majestic austere beauty of the passing mountains
in shades of green, grey, and gold;
it lies quietly absorbing the scents and sounds of the valley.
The driver stops in a tiny village for a chai and a smoke
while passengers stretch their legs,
the stop a brief respite for their weary bones.
The post bag rubs shoulders with sacks
of sweet green peas meant for the urban markets.
The thickets of pink flowers wave prettily
but the bus speeds past its destination in mind.
In Manali, the post waits in a back room
of a large building to be sorted.
A postwoman separates the cards
which seemed to cling together;
parted and divided and sorted,
they lie in their lonely little compartments,
another bus journey to be endured to Chandigarh
and then train journeys to the south, east and west.
Hikkim and Spiti, a forgotten past,
the cards are traversing a different path.
It's no more mountains, but the plains,
no more inclines but flats.
No bright stars strewn across a clear sky,
but an enduring grey that obscures the atmosphere.

And finally, a card travels to Bangalore and its outskirts.
A little piece of Spiti in Kengeri.

PRAGYA BAJPAI
Media, War, And Peace

Dear Media,

Talk about the simmering conflict in Ukraine or Ethiopia
Talk about war or settling a thousand scores
in Vietnam, Russia, France, or different parts of Asia

Talk about endless enmity, hatred
But don't call it pointless
Create propaganda and hide potential threats
Talk about annexation of territories
and hide personal interest
Glorify ideology, faculty, power, dignity
But don't say: forgive and forget
To hell with unrest in the country
To hell with mental effects

Fight for resources and exploit them too
Fight for development and destroy them too
Talk about crisis of food and all global issues
But to hell with the poor and the future of the youth

Talk about colliding galaxies and existing chaos
Pollute the minds and don't let them know
Fill the hearts that crave for more
They will be thankful for the first-hand info
But don't mention if it's worth living or dying for

Talk about skirmishes, talk about conflicts
After all, it's not yet a war,
and definitely not your responsibility at all
Until some miracle happens and the world is at peace
You focus on TRPs

Yours truly,
A Citizen of Every Country

The Beast

In the midst of Breaking News
showing violence, attacks, killings
in war-torn countries
with bold rolling headlines on the screen
about exploitation of conflict dynamics,
about party politics,
about fragility, complexity, strategy,
their views on global solidarity
that I watched intently
with nipping unease

My puppy suddenly threw himself at me
straight on to my breast,
buried his head against my belly,
refusing to watch terrifying humanity
I heard him moan, turn his tail, feeling frail

He was scared, fearful in shape
I held him tight and said,
We are living in a world we can't escape
and with dismayed eyes wide open
he pleaded for sympathy like men
stuck in refugee camps

So I turned it off for his peace of mind
The breaking news broke us both
He didn't know what it was, but
demanded amity in his own tongue
and showed me who the real beast is

KIRAN BHAT
A Loud Noise Asked

A loud noise asked:
When will you find peace?
Kiran says:
I ought to stop listening to what my family says.
First, I will be able to listen to myself.
Then, my purpose will come.
Then, I will follow my purpose.
Then, I will know peace.

Previously published in *Speaking in Tongues* (Red River, July 2022)

The President Asks

The president asks: How is freedom in our country?

Kiran says:
When the lobster is thrust into boiling water,
He doesn't know his circumstance.
He simply has his legs and claws tied up.
Perhaps he knows his destiny.
Most likely he does not.

The lobster is thrown into the boiling water.
The lid is put on top.
He looks on the other side of the translucent lid.
He imagines the islands,
the fat fish of his thrill.

And then he stops thinking.

Kiran concludes: Whether or not we have freedom, I
am not sure.
My brain has long been boiled.

Previously published in *Speaking in Tongues* (Red River, July 2022)

A Reporter Asked

A reporter asked; Aren't you worried about the times
we live in?

Kiran responds; Of course, I worry!
We are losing so many cultures, so much land.
Day by day it's getting hotter.
Peninsulas are becoming islands.

And the news isn't giving us information,

It's suffocating us.

But I am also excited about our future.
We have reached a point where Chinese people care
what happens in Kenya.
But there are now Chinese people caring about what
happens in Kenya.
That fact itself is encouraging.

We are truly beginning to care about each other,
And this is part of the way.

Previously published in *Speaking in Tongues* (Red River, July 2022)

ANINDITA BOSE
Peace Blooms In Silence

Some of us do not belong to this
world
we travel for a while to observe
the way this world moves back
and forth

Perhaps we are sent to know
that the lifetime of a human is
not enough to understand the
essence of living and breathing

We observe, we feel, we wonder
why there are so many spaces
and blanks between the words
and the actions of people

Perhaps we are sent to witness
that dreams and realities are
mere illusions, and we need to
accept everything that revolves
around us

I wonder, what we shall do and
finally, what will happen to us
who are here on earth only to
see and not take part in the flow
of time…

Are we on the map of the universe
or are we invisible beings, waiting
for some miracle to guide us to our
final destiny?

Some of us do not belong to this
world
we are the air, fire, water, and earth
itself
we are born to sacrifice ourselves
for the ecstasy of humanity

Shakti Flows Through Memories

It's *maha ashtami* again

three years now, in the journey
of life

the lonely daughter waits alone
in hope that time could walk
backwards…

people linger around
family grows but when a mother
leaves the world, darkness fills
each day like a broken bottle of
ink on white empty papers.

On earth, sometimes people are
forgetful

they do not remember that future
kills the past and the present is a
reflection of life.

and that fleeting moment holds
the truth that we need to embrace
those who are destined to be with
us…

The daughters, and sometimes
mothers too, wish that they did
not belong to each other
while the universe weaves their
fates in silence.

maha ashtami: one of the most auspicious days of the Durga Puja festival

ISHMEET KAUR CHAUDHRY
The Road To My Home

The road to my home
has many twists and turns
it also has fences and walls
at places where it nears the borders
it has barbed wires too

The road to my home
has many colours and shapes
it is also steep and rough
at places it is muddy brown and dusty
it has a lot of potholes too

The road to my home
is torn and broken
it is also neglected and ignored
at places there are check-posts
it has a lot of police too

But the road to my home
despite the turns and the twists
despite many colours and shapes
despite being torn and broken
leads to the most peaceful place on this Earth

The road to my home with fences and walls
despite being steep and rough
despite being neglected and ignored
leads to the place where the embodiment of love and joy
my grandmother, still lives

This road to my home
takes us to our roots
to our stories and songs
to the hot springing tea and
a lot of love spurring from my grandmother's eyes

The borders and the barbed wires
the muddy potholes
the check-posts with a lot of police
do not stop us from reaching this place, our home
where peace flows in my grandmother's veins

RONALD TUHIN D'ROZARIO
Endings And Beginnings

How it dropped a pause
Shifting Berlin between the fingers?
Baisakh is the frothy mouth of sea,
Galloping hooves in a war fed appetite.

Führerbunker's suicide explores the migraine of
homecoming,
In the sermon of a fallen might—
The calculus of nose,
Hangs a moustache guarding a pimpled grin.

A blue curtain of conspiracy in the maternity ward of
April—
The obstetrician's table of chatter
paws the belly like a hungry cat,
A premature birth is a misprint
Sniffing a window of rain in anaesthesia.

Nearby a middleclass lane
A childhood swallows the church bell of hiccups
Crisis is the anthology of all lives mattered,
Beneath the flesh or at his father's territory—dimly lit,
Where a virgin mother weeps over her dead son.

The full moon's night falls off the ribs to a bull-face yawn
Sex-starved. Stubborn. Orthodox,
The body a migrant dictionary of apology,
Buckles its needs to the unemployed waist.

In the yard of a blocked artery paddles the heart,
It rumbled to crow-a-crow game—
possessed in a breath of cyanide.

His shadow guides the rusty nozzle of a gun,
Whipped on the cold chin of absence
The neighbour's house grinds to dust.

An agency of flies flocks his slender and greasy throat,
Stealing letters in hieroglyphs with lost addresses—
A borrowed desk of scars.

There is a man nameless as a misfit tree,
holding your summer solstice upon his shoulders—

There is a man eaten in the lamp lit hour.

Baisakh: A month of the Hindu calendar that corresponds to April/May in the
Gregorian calendar
Führerbunker: An air raid shelter located near the Reich Chancellery in Berlin,
Germany; it was the last of the Führer Headquarters used by Adolf Hitler
during World War II
Previously published in *Madras Courier* (April 16, 2022)

The Otherness Of Belonging

And when autumn burns ripe
murmuring as a sage,
I do not hate them anymore,
In a burst of wildflower faces,
Return forgotten afternoons and wall
hangings
Forlorn. Forbidden. Forgotten.
Wearing a torn foot of yesterday.

Into a frozen city on the mirror,
the storm keepers of the native
Exhale a lung full of voices,
Their unbuttoned shirts smuggle
across the windmill of flesh,
Sprawling the faded acres along:
Shoulder stitch, armpits, cuffs, and collar—
Drown on a voyage to the sea.
Crisis is a sad cactus plant in a
live-in-relationship to belonging—
A rag of honour. A name. A heartbeat
It is then the sun falls over the eyes
Squashing the orange of its
sleeplessness,
Fondness grows into a silent forest.

The lips submit to the address of the
other,
Letting the kite chasers and night
growers belong, *Ghare-Baire.*

Ghare-Baire: A 1984 Bengali film directed by Satyajit Ray; based on
Rabindranath Tagore's novel of the same name
Previously published in *Outlook India* (May 01, 2022)

Jasmine

What makes the night a prison?
Rolling its tongue up the sleeve.
A city like an urchin, unsettled—
Reserves a birth in the ovary of Jasmine
Mewling and sucking its saggy breasts.

Petals flower the newborn's head,
Your eyes of names crawls on a subtle summer's
afternoon—
In the memory of a frothy green sea—is a man,
missing from the spine of Eros.
His anatomy is the diagram of your child,
Into a parched womb of an open mouth
A restless wind on his hair sweeps the generation of
famine.

Loneliness of earth grows in white,
Grief. Virtue. Worship—
and now a litany of flower,
Fragrance is a time bomb ticking in the teacup,
Between wild months on calendar.
The Jasmine's head—
Fallen naked over your thumb

Eats the raw abstinence of skin,
The perennial of time crashes over and over again.

Autonomy of your body is a harbour
Ships and men slit like rocks
And the binary of eclipse on the wall,
Stand in guard as the president's men.

Sleep articulates the language of a hoar in darkness—
Preparing a recipe on the kitchen stove
The bedouins come selling yawns,
Stacking pillows of guilt in the heart
Branching silence and dead Jasmine.

Previously published in *The Pangolin Review* (Issue 19, June 22, 2021)

RAYJI DE GUIA
Rosas
after *Emiliana Kampilan*

Binibini, I used to
   call you—from that song
we couldn't forget: a kundiman
    to soothe the afternoon until
      Lola turns the station to pray
rosary for absence of news
   before she herself succumbed
       to grief. An orchestra, a choir,
   or a waltz, we danced
     as lady and another
   lady as man. Beneath
moonshine, I open my eyes
   not to twirl out of your arms
but to take up arms in the country—
     side unreachable. Binibini, I still call
      you in my mind, a ballroom
   for the eternal encore
     before our parting. As women
coming of age, starry-eyed
   in spite of war, the promised
last dance keeps the beating

of my feet across fields, over
mountains, praying for that day
I follow the steps back to you.
On that day, a song will begin,
as scriptures have promised, but
of trumpeting jazz and disco.
I will find you in the chanting
crowd, among comrades, blood-red petals
on the streets. Halina, binibini, I'll beckon,
hand-in-hand, we'll dance the swing
before their effigies
aflame. A fulfilment
of retribution.

binibini: Filipino for "miss" or "lady"; generally refers to unmarried women
lola: Filipino for "grandmother"
kundiman: a genre of traditional Filipino love songs; the lyrics are written in Tagalog
halina: Filipino for "come here"

New Creation

Hailed as god he drops the word: Bodies
fall one by one, not by force of gravity
   but by the whims of a few; a command as easy
         as pointing at a star in any galaxy.
Which is to say there may not be enough
   of us for the downpour of meteors
   and meteorites into our sky.
      Tell your friends and their friends,
            tell the children and their parents
                  the horrors,
                  but do not stop
         when they have sunk into a void.
      Pull them up, whisper of love,
   and bring them out in the sun
because when we chant our hopes,
      a new universe unfolds from each syllable,
            and the aftermath will outlive us.

War
after *Incendies* (2010)

In times of war, what is   the worst
that can   become of me? Is it   death
     of my son   family   or
lover?   When I fight to avenge
what has been taken from me   choose
a side   seek a cause   to shelter my grief
     what is the sanction for my actions?
For fighting against   men   who fight
     men against them,   there is no place
for me, this is   my transgression:
     to be a woman in times of war.
In this country, the worst   is not to be killed
     it is to be raped   again   and again
until I break—   but remember, the president
should go first.   If that does not work,
     then to be shot   with a rifle
up my vagina   because that
          is where he finds
     our humanity.

KABIR DEB
Navigation

I am thinking to start
a new job, a very basic home
of entrepreneurs where for
everything they make
they'd be given the chance to meet
the people of marginalized areas,
and to speak to them in their
language, they'd have to
stay in their homes to understand
how they live by looking towards
the Saturn they've never seen
and expecting a piece of
bread they'll never have, they must
know all of these, the core
of my civilisation lies in
them, their meat now
smells of my ascendancy, mine is
made up of their sacrifices,
in short, I need to atone
for what I've with me.

A sky breaks upon
them when we converse on

how to romance for the
next forty years of
my life, they sell
onions to us as a vegetable we
need as an extra, they on the
other hand, have a spice as
happiness and a potato as a hope
of a good sleep, I can still hear
them banging their heads
before the God that'll never listen,
as we walk round and round
our dining table to serve the best
meal we make, I see a lady
feeding milk that is made
up of conflict, chaos, a corrupted
culture of conditioning.

I won't have an office
just a river of buses,
they'd slow down before every
hut that speaks of exploitation,
somewhere a man would be caged
for beating his wife, a girl would
be given the hope to coexist
with everyone, the widows
would be provided the chance
to explore what their body wants
irrespective of how they should
be, I've seen the townies
lynch a man right by his phallus
for carrying what he had been
born with, a life, a choice
to be what this nature wanted

him to be, a man who loved the
love of his life in the body of
another man, it'd be the
job of the entrepreneurs to stall
the flag of hope so high that
the kites could scream a
song of win from top!

Godliness...!

Go for small moments
watch a grasshopper nibble a grass
touch the water that rolls down
the stem of a plant, keep it over its leaf and
watch how it balances the droplet using
the breeze, there's a lot to learn from
them for they do not demand a thing in return.

Watch the labour feed
his young child using his efforts to
know how even the poorest ones
can avoid complaining just to leave these
tantrums to someone they don't know,
he might do good, he might do bad,
he might be useless, but to him he's a friend.

Renounce your post
that absorbs all your sweat for just
a swollen wallet, avoid a mid-life
crisis by sleeping at least four nights in a
week beneath the stars, watch how they
hold a meaning in your life, these tiny
things matter when everything is too large.

Ask an orphan how
does it feel to have the company of that
middle-aged beggar who sings the
folk songs of Sundarbans, you'd know that
the orphan is the sole audience he gets,
and he's the sole friend who invests
an hour of love for an entire day of bullying.

This world thrives
on the surface of a coffee table where
two people are trying to be in each
other's lives, it resides in that old cricket that
is a witness of how even after some riot,
some crazy people arrive to clean
the blood, and the butterfly flies over death.

We did not choose
to be a part of this world where we're
made to focus on a story that isn't
even ours, we feel the world resides in them,
and all we do is to work on the benefits
of being pretentious, however, where
we live is in thoughts and our loud silence.

Find a place where
you can sell your dreams just to check
their price, then if you wish you can
store them as antiques, yeah, you'd be valued,
life is a good conspiracy, and it isn't bad
to live, one just has to hold it tightly
and smile for no reason, it needs madness!

Crumbling Chaos

It is not time I know
but still do inform
me when the walls would
crumble, I've to see the
people behind them,
I'm sure they look like me,
sit and love their loved ones
like most of us do, I don't
want to see what they
read, I am not worthy
enough to decode words.

I do want to know where do
they keep their flowers,
how dirty are their hands
of the mud we speak
of in our meetings,
I'm sure I won't have to
attend any other to solve the
riddle of where we'd end
if we do certain things,
and how monstrous
we've to have to become
to share the same sky!

Feel free to hammer
my head, it has seen a lot to
find solace in eating the
remains of the million
deaths everyone dies, it
has been nailed like a locust
and severed like a goat,
it has died on death,
I just want to see everything
ruined, everyone broken,
the world would then have a
hymn, it'd be of a bee, of a
breaking bud, a rotting order,
and an ovulating chaos,
I know I'd see all of these
behind those tall walls.

SONIA DOGRA
The White Poppy And Its Twin

A white poppy scatters like wind,
laughs like rolling pebbles, paints
from a palette of rainbow colours
floating on palms of seashell angels.

The white poppy's twin rains like fire,
soles hurting, a dizziness rising in its
belly, slowly nauseating the senses.

The white poppy wallows in the scent
of the night blooming cereus, cuddles
blue-brown bruises, knows how to fill
gaping holes in lonely hearts.

The twin wanders weary, losing its way
in a maze of red. A whirlwind of darkness
drowns the moon in a rushing current.

The white poppy discovers subtle pangs
of hurt hanging in waves in the air, builds
ways out of nasty, gilded cages, is nice to
the saddest symphonies, even affectionate.

The twin drags a sea of humanity, their breaths
laden with dust, poetries contorted, tied into knots,
dipped in blood. Cold, even rusted.

The poppy opens its petals beyond borders,
a white canopy bounces up and down;
decodes the language of flowers on velvety
grass. Chooses love.

The twin treads like a vulture on a barren
mountain. By the cemetery, scores of gravediggers
wait past the setting sun.

Anjali G. Sharma
The Obscured Ubiquitous

The stillness and serenity;
Of the untouched and unscarred;
A promise; an anticipation.
A word which is given.

The tumult; the tempest,
Tides of doubt;
The demons of conceit;
Overwhelm, cloud, and weaken.

Not a secret, but widely known.
The melting, the deliquesce;
From that touch,
That soothing word.
That harmony within.

Its power immense;
Every hour and each moment,
From the surface to its core,
It's pristine and encompasses all.

The light of compassion,
The touch of kindness,

The thread of peace;
For it, only a crevice is sufficient
To make its way up and metamorphose.

Before it radiates outwards;
It has to travel within
For there is no path which leads to it,
For it is a path for everything.

Its sensitivity is the power,
Spirit universal;
Nature ubiquitous;
Yet in the humdrum,
Is easily forgotten.
Something which is
To be cherished,
and celebrated;
This and every moment!

RAHUL GAUR
I Am Sorry

I am sorry.
I really am.

I am sorry for the little child
who waited and writhed in hunger,
while our saviours,
in their ivory towers,
lay with their bellies full
in a deep slumber.

I am sorry,
oh, old lady,
because you waited,
while tears dried up
on your cheeks,
for the one who would never return:
he—your son,
and the frantic crowds
in the distance,
smeared in his blood,
danced in fun.

I am sorry
for you—the poor man.
Barefoot you trudged along,
searching for the promised land,
and your blood wet the ground,
and your sweat,
and the world raved and chanted
about the deeds
of our leaders great.

I am sorry
for me,
because I waited and watched,
as they cried for help
and their eyes begged of me
to stop.

I laughed at my helplessness.
And then I cried.
For all of you—mankind,
because I was sorry,
and I still am.
I still am.

ANUJA GHIMIRE
Homophily

Soon enough, he, too will remain a quiet picture
The clean sneakers, red shirt,
and shorts on a sleeping toddler
As the tides run him over
on the border of land and water
His eyes closed and nose squished on the shore's
shelter
While we hug our children tighter
and wish their futures brighter
Our conscience losing the anchor, afloat and washing
up, lighter and lighter

Previously published in *Dove, an Anthology of Peace* (November 2019)

Odessa

Jaha na pahuche ravi
Waha pahuche kavi

Where sun cannot reach
There poet arrives

Ganesh, you cannot fit in my eyes
men wheel you first to the prayer hall, centre, stage
drumbeat cannot sit in my heart
we clap in the air and near our knees
circle, left foot front, back step, right foot front
dear god, I've chanted your 108 names
Ganesh in Texas, Ganesh in 2019
we pray loud
Ganesh, the baby boy wails
dear son of Shiva, the toddler won't sit on the floor
when we lift open palms to the ceiling
Ganesh, I didn't fast before I came to see you
O, one who absorbs all obstacles
O, holy, holy light
my daughters forgot and sat with their backs to you
but they sang your name
dear god, I am afraid
the ghee-lit prayers are not enough

Previously published in *Crack the Spine* (November 2019)

NAVNEET GREWAL
The Peace Saga

a name lost from every dictionary
alphabets just do not consent
an arduous rhythm
barred bare by language

historians plead to its charm
dynasties wiped out in its pursuit
monuments stripped of glory
families left wailing

a syntax error of minds
with vanity underlined to quote
the ego of a few delirious
will hammer the homes of many

it is not extinct but veiled
under human virtues
let every being whisper its cries
let peace prevail to numb the noise

The Dulcet Dub

Splints varied exist
In the rolls of wicker unbound
Each shred holds a different story
Of being and believing a part
We spell harmony
In smaller compartments of hope
Together the symphony allures
As we hold ours, as the most unrequited
Shunning the self to realise the whole
The preamble of peace beckons all
Not only doves, the *Corvus*, the sparrow, the cuckoo
A trill in the unison of humankind true
This armistice of acceptance
Nip in the bud the giant of selfish credence
That bloats with greed uncouth
Let each home revel in content
Conflate a dulcet felicity
Gossamer weaves the world unfolds
As the talisman of serenity flows

SHRUTI HAJIRNIS GUPTE
Mahabharatee
five women who held court before the war

While the stars are growing dim
The world of darkness is lightened with a beam

Here comes Satyavati with an absolute resolution
The great destructive war must not happen

Destruction can be caused as the result of action
But peace can be brought only through discussion

Before the men start fighting at sunrise
Satyavati calls forth four women great and wise

Will she be able to bring peaceful settlement
Not sure, but discussion will be pacifying enlightenment

No one wants war, we all love peace
But what about the fact that war is a reprisal for injustice

For thirteen years Draupadi has burned in the fire of revenge
What will be the fate of her adamantine pledge

Only war can avenge her miserable humiliation
A society that causes injustice to a woman is doomed to destruction

But Draupadi stands accused of being selfish in the court of Satyavati
Gandhari is against war and silent is Mata Kunti

Rukmini reaches the court, and she is convinced
It is not always a woman who has to sacrifice

All are bound to our actions in the past
Sometimes war is the only outcome at last

War that transforms is a fire sacrifice, a sacred one
Where the device, the object, the doer, and the act, all are one

For envy and enmity let the men fight
But with a great detachment let women unite

So set at peace are the five Mahabharatee
With wisdom of life that brings equanimity

RIZA HASLAM
We Live In A World Of Collectiveness

A piece of your kindness,
A bit of my goodness,
Creates a chunk of benevolence.
For this is the secret of a harmonious relationship.
Malice can break a bond and even damage a
connection,
But the power of solidarity can bridge
the gap of camaraderie.
Together we can do more, hand in hand
we can bring peace.
Your judgement I may oppose;
My cleverness you may question,
Yet we can act in one accord.
And how do we achieve this? With unity.
For we deserve a world of peace, freedom, and
harmony
Just as we have the right to equality and liberty.
With compassion there is humanity.
Yet without it there is but cruelty.
With consideration there is humility;
Yet without it there is but vanity.
We may have different nationalities,

Yet we are one collectively.
Each one of us can make the world a better place.
We live in a world of collectiveness.
May we utilise the power to contribute
To purposeful social change.
In doing so, the daunting idea of a peaceful world
Is as easy as ABC.
Let us find motives to commend;
Never will we strike for reasons to criticise.
When we feel the urge to vilify,
Let us hold our grip.
When we find ourselves in adoration,
Let us shout for joy.
When we are tempted to accuse,
Let us divert our attention.
When we are treated with respect,
Let us reciprocate in return.
In doing so, we acknowledge humanity,
And respect individualities.
We live in a world of collectiveness.
And how must we collaborate?
From now on we must act in kindness.
We must show empathy to all mankind
And release all bitterness from our system.
From this day on, we must take the first step
To accomplish this goal.
With resilience we must grow,
With patience we must become.

SEEMA JAIN
Survival In A War Zone

While exploring the mysterious secrets of human anatomy
and learning to heal any aberrations in its systems;
in the evenings, sauntering around
the glitzy shopping malls,
the busy streets throbbing with hustle and bustle,
the well-structured lanes of the beautiful city,
the huge skyscrapers standing tall in their majesty,
singing of man's limitless glory

Couldn't imagine life would do such a quick somersault,
so unpredictably, hardly allowing time to escape;
hard to believe we would have
to forget about our usual classes,
missing one of which was a serious fault till yesterday

Then, we heard the sounds of sirens day and night
and had to rush to underground bunkers
to escape the onslaught of bombs, missiles, rockets,
the billowing columns of smoke and dragon-like fires,
engulfing buildings, roads, houses, people;
the sparrows and squirrels baffled and confused,
or roasted alive in the ensuing infernos

Those same streets where music, fragrance, and laughter
emanated from jovial folks once
witnessed caravans of men, women,
little kids, and the elderly
fleeing their homes to some unknown
uncharted *safer* destination
dragging along a few belongings and reluctant children,
stupefied at being pushed away
from their dear homes and friends,
their favourite toys and games,
their schools, and playmates,
walking on foot for miles, with snow falling
in sub-zero temperatures

The business of survival in
a war zone is no laughing matter, you see
forget about your homes, or food or water, dear friends;
looking at those who went out to buy
groceries and never came back,
you should be glad to be still alive
in the midst of mayhem all around.

Does victory in war prove one side right or wrong?
Do thousands and millions who die,
are rendered homeless, not count?
When will nations learn of other ways
to settle their scores?
When will survival of humans take precedence
over egos, greed, and arrogance?
When, O when?

O For A Pinch Of Pixie Dust

O for a pinch of pixie dust
that could make life an unending bliss
that could usher in a change of heart
transform this world
into a land of peace and love
dissolving all hatred and strife

O for a pinch of pixie dust
that could be gently sprinkled
over gun-toting monsters
out on a senseless killing spree
piercing toothless milky smile with bayonets,
forcing mothers, sisters, daughters to hide,
in gutter holes to escape disgrace,
unleashing a reign of catastrophe and horror!

O for a pinch of pixie dust
that could eliminate
terror hanging mid-air like crematorium smoke
an eerie silence lurking over deserted houses' parapets,
with people reeling constantly under
the cold shadow of death!

O for a pinch of pixie dust
that could soothe and embalm
human lives traumatised, liberties threatened,
children orphaned, women widowed,
men caught up in the eye of storm
knowing not whither to go!

O for a pinch of pixie dust
that could bring rejuvenating showers,
wash away tears from anguished eyes
and fears from tormented hearts,
that could forge deep bonds of healing love
unifying the divide between man and man
making this life blissful for all!

Previously published in *Pixie Dust & All Things Magical: Global Poetry in English* (ed. Anita Nahal, Authorspress, January 2022)

The Splintered Pigeon

The freshly bathed vast expanse
of the green grassy lawn in a park
on a moist drizzly morning,
and near one of its pavements,
lay a tiny pigeon, unconscious.

The fitness freaks briskly sauntered around
on the circular gravel and concrete pathways:
some with earphones plugged,
enjoyed music devotional;
some rapt in the throes of a motivational talk,
looked around unseeing,
unmindful of the wounded pigeon
writhing in pain.

And within the blink of an eye
a hungry dog emerged from nowhere.
Like a thunderbolt, it fell upon its hapless prey,
pounced upon it, ripped it apart,
and digging into its entrails,
scattered its splintered feathers all over
the dew-covered green glistening grass.

NEERA KASHYAP
The Tree Of Life

The eagle's eye, aerial and fiery
gazes down from the treetop stretching to heaven
at the outstretched intertwined branches
of relationships—
old new burgeoning twisted gnarled.
It observes:
Their power in the earth of their growth,
decay, death and re-birth.
In the joy and pain of photosynthesis
In the ever-changing seasons of desire and expectation
In the fluctuating winds of love and support
In the winter of sorrow and unfulfillment
when the mother tree withdraws her nutrients
and rusting leaves add theirs to her roots—
letting go, falling to the ground.

During storms, the eagle sees the drama of our
projections;
our loves and hates,
our recognitions,
our seasonal withdrawals,
our assimilations.

Our growing peace when there is no wish for change.
Just an acceptance of creation, its hidden roots of
flowing water.
The whole reflective of the light and love of heaven.

The eagle swoops down to carry heavenwards
the snake hidden in the tree's aqueous roots
in its powerful talons
wondering if its waters are immortal.

Previously published in *World Inkers Network* (June 2022)

The Call

My forefathers heard the call of
the *murshid* in their veins—
ancient blood and stardust flowed as one.
They followed their blood, sometimes to earth's end,
sometimes to the next village
till the call became a form, the form a teacher
and Time stood still.

I am a different kind of nomad—
hearing the call of a different bloodflow;
they call me 'minority'.
In reality a scapegoat, a scapegoat to
a need for revenge
in the others, the majority—
so they feel shored up against their own suffering.
'Let the bastard suffer so I don't.
Let the rat die so there's no threat to ME.'
It keeps my mind moving, throbbing, hurting, raging
to the ancient drumbeat of bigotry, sectarianism, war.
The beat pulses correspondingly in majority minds
below the threshold of the conscious,
where threats could be real or imagined;
flaring up in the collective as flashpoints—

fomenting isolation, feeding tension, fueling assault.
For the illusion of security,
for the illusion of approval of a community.

Beneath my turbulent veins
I hear my forefathers call—
I just about hear it.
It is a call for prayer and forgiveness,
a song of love for their *murshid,*
a song of love for one another,
for Nature and for poetry
in submission to the *murshid,*
in submission to our own oneness.

murshid: Urdu for "instructor" or "guide"
Previously published in *Verse of Silence* (Summer Issue, 2019)

Tree Woman

It's the tree she holds
with one arm, the other looped
around a branch in flower—
her sinuous nakedness in *tribhanga* pose.

She is the tree.

The tree woman in full flower
nests birds, animals, insects
fragrances in her blood red bark.
Music moves through her with the wind,
sonorous as a storm,
gentle as a lilt,
eternal as ocean tides.
From her deep shade, every creature
listens,
to the flowing sap of flowering,
as blood seeps through her bark,
as blood sings through her leaves.

In sculptures, she is small, her leaves large,
her nurturing undiminished.

Ancients say when a woman reaches up to touch a branch,
the tree bursts into flower.

tribhanga: a stance used in traditional Indian classical dance forms, where the body bends in one direction at the knees, the other at the hips and then the other again at the shoulders and neck
Previously published in *The Well-Earned* (ed. Kiriti Sengupta, Hawakal Publishers, August 2022)

Gopal Lahiri
Resolve

I only need to close my eyes,
amid the sound of music, low lights and jostling
the whole evening
collapses in the tone of the magic,
in the steins of the coffee cup and saucer,
vapours decorated with red flames.

I look and I see outside,
the wooden bridge that does not bear and
the God that does not yield,
The fanatic and apostle cry about religion,
much elaborate, much precise.
a voice like a stifled drum reaches me.

I can now see trees beyond,
leaves floating in an ochre light,
I listen to a voice that travels through me,
the voice of resolve and resolution,
passing over the noises of life,
I imagine the tribune of a people in peace and harmony.

Harmony

Come to my shore.

The random hands, the curious looks are ready to
build the wall of dreams.

Each one of us stands before the flickering flame
from these shades of grey and grey, in the end
the moving lamps light the shadow.

You don't know what is there and also is
the blackness of space.

The time lives through, some of us there,
none of us fight in the changing landscape.

We will walk for peace, for amity.

A new gaze, a new thought, a new
collection of moments.

sounds, images, words—all combine
to build a whole world.

We dream another sun, another newness in the world.

World Peace

Now that the wind surrenders,

I will never live in that world that carries
blood stains and bullet holes under the sleeves

the oppressive skies go to hiding,
the enemy's hand weakens,
lies do not exist anymore.
those hungry children filling the canvas
come out in the open, under the new sunlight.

In my world, the landscape and the farmland

that has been held back for years,
and kept secret is now free.
all the hidden letters
of life slip out of the dust and haze
erasing those scared faces, those empty eyes,

I want to stand on my tiptoes
and ready to play around.

more leaves, more green forest,
more beds of fresh grass,

flocks of birds get larger over
the huts and fields of corn
the flowers blossom in quietude,

child on the chest and listen to mother's song
that drifts her towards the rest.

I love to see that refuge, that sanctuary.

MEENAKSHI M. SINGH
The Unapologetic Dance

Sometimes she gets scared
Of the erupting lava of truth
Gushing out of her being
The threatening burst
Collapsing the rigid structures around

And she shudders and stops
To avoid the fingers pointed
Covers herself with every possible layer
Silence, Submission, Subjugation
To alienate from chameleons
Who distort everything that's good
She ever believed in
That world of hypocrites

She sneaks into an alternate realm
A world of her love
Where they say what they feel
Then and there
All travel light
They dance and yes, they fight

A world of absolute nakedness
Where there aren't any veils
An ecstatic tribe celebrating the now
A world where they don't measure
Her worth, her big trunk

Where they don't measure
The length of her skirt
Her claim to be an heir
The days, years and her lifetime
Where she flows careless being a waterfall
Not knowing which river, she merges into
She just flows and dances
Ecstatic, being unapologetic

ANJU MAKHIJA
Vanishing Words

Let go of the moment, it never was yours,
never will be. Stockpile the papers,
turn on the tap, till the ink bleeds.
till blood feels like water,
flowing easily between
impervious niches.
Let our internal
confabulations
weave the
joy of
nihility.

Butterball

An enormous round boulder,
perfectly balanced
an eyeball on a pin head.

Four Gods, carved in stone,
stare wide-eyed, bewildered.

Phantom-like fishing boats
stranded in the sea,
submerged pagodas
appear and disappear.

I've been here before,
felt the permanence of Gods,
permanence of stone.

The equilibrium comes
from other-worldly terrains.

Krishna's gigantic Butterball is a granite rock resting on a sharp incline. It is located in the coastal town of Mamallapuram, Tamil Nadu, India

Baffled

The truth is within us,
then why does it hide?
                    O Lord.

Birds in the sky,
wine cups, gallows,
symbols delude,
metaphors confuse.

Stars remain unchanged,
lava erupts in our veins,
saliva sucks venom.

Sprouted, I split like a bean,
half of me endeavours,
half of me observes.

Apple tempts in new ways,
Samsung dictates our lives,
Google peers down the iris.

I can go on and on.
Please discharge batteries,
unplug my adapter,

switch off my thoughts.
I will merge,
or emerge insane.

Shall I surrender
and simply love you
like a child?

O Lord.

VINEETHA MOKKIL
After The War

After the war
They planted peace
In scarred fields
Shoots sprouted, tender green
Peaches blushed on the branches
Apples bloomed red again
Parrots, chirping
circled the droneless skies
The blood moon shed its stains
and shone, milky white
Stars came out of hiding
to heal the wounded skies.

Guns fell silent
Barbed wire fences
stopped drawing blood
The night, sighing, slipped
into restful sleep
The day grew quiet
So quiet sometimes you could
hear a butterfly's wings flap.

After the war
They planted peace
The first harvest
They offered to the Gods
And the ghosts
of those they had lost
Memory watered the land
Memory whispered in the wind
Memory a prayer
A blessing, a curse
A sign, pulsing
In the summer sun, the winter dark.

After the war they wept bitter tears
After the war they tended peace.

ANKIT RAJ OJHA
Mahanadi

If only I knew I was marrying a baby!
She taunts me, laughing as she gets in
the front seat of her father's Honda Activa,
signalling at me to hop behind.

I don't know how to ride a two-wheeler.
I have been too busy studying, watching
superhero cinema, playing gigs with my band,
fending off my inevitable male-pattern baldness—
a gift from my father's side.

I have managed to retain my apical pride all the way
into my third decade, beating Papa's and Baba's genes
so far, but have missed out on knowing how it feels
to be sitting in the driver's seat of a motorcycle—
the mundane thrill of feeling a rush of air
coursing through the vegetation on the head
is an adventure to me.

This morning in Cuttack is no different as I sit on
the back seat feeling second-hand wind kissing
the Mahanadi and in turn rustling my hair that have
long outstayed their welcome.

She parks at a petrol pump and senses instantly my
unease at stopping in a remote spot amidst
rough-looking men.
She puts me at ease, saying there's nothing to worry, for this
is Odisha, her home turf, where they have
a festival to worship menstruating women, and where
most men are dark only in skin.

We resume with a full tank, the riverside road stretching
forever with the Mahanadi, like the Mahanadi.
The trees are the deepest shade of green, appearing
almost fake as if painted twice over.

We stop for coconut water. The *nariyal waala* cracks open
sunroofs in two coconuts in less than half a dozen strikes,
puts in straws, and we're good to go.

I follow her up a small flight of stairs onto a river view point
peppered with shy married couples
and brazen unmarried ones.

As I gaze in awe at the sprawling blue waters
(blue to the point of disbelief)
and try in vain to hide my hair in a bandana
from the damp river wind, she recounts simpler days
from her childhood, of how on Sunday mornings her father
would take her to buy fresh handpicked fish and prawns
from the riverside, and how their pampered cow named *Cow*
would run the entire household.

The choicest dairy products,
milk for the fish in the pond to grow fat on,
manure from cow dung,

cow dung cakes for cooking fuel,
biogas to power the home and the vehicles, and more.
Maybe *this* is why they call an *animal*
Mother, not for some mythic magic tale.

I listen intently, growing content at how she relishes
the tales featuring fish and crabs and prawns
and her grandma's cooking pot.
I am a vegetarian, yet I do not flinch at her graphic description.
We have an understanding.
She'll never ask me to eat meat, and I'll never keep her
from her native food preference.

Fearing that her tales must have made me suffer,
she drives us to a vegetarian tiffin point by the river.
The pot-bellied shop owner is amused at my broken Odia
and asks her if I am not from around here.
She tells him I'm from Bihar and he is delighted,
recounting his time as a soldier stationed in my home state,
and quickly unloading on our plate another serving
of hot spicy *ghughuni* despite our protests.

The bill comes to 25 rupees, nothing compared to what
I am used to spending on a decent breakfast in the north.
I almost feel bad for the ex-soldier who sells food this good
this cheap, and am instantly overcome with shame at
having allowed the patronising thought to creep in.

She is about to hit ignition when she is distracted by
a cow mooing beside her and a dog tugging at her feet.
She descends as if to greet and reunite
with a long forgotten memory.

The dog gobbles a dozen *idlis*, the cow four times that much.
We ride back home on the dreamy Mahanadi road,
she transported to her history, I smiling ear to ear
at having spent way more than what I usually do on breakfast.

nariyal waala: Hindi for "coconut seller"
ghughuni: a curry made of peas, chickpeas, or Bengal gram, originating in the
Eastern Indian states of Bihar, Jharkhand, West Bengal, and Odisha
idli: a savoury rice cake originating in Southern India and Sri Lanka,
prepared by steaming a fermented batter of rice and black lentils
Previously published in *Pinpricks* (Hawakal Publishers, June 2022)

Reflections Upon Visiting The Old Cemetery In Roorkee

I hold her by the waist
as she perches
precariously on the thin
brick protruding out
of the boundary wall,
grabbing the iron rails
with her life as she tries
to steal glimpses of the dead.
Can't see a thing!
She heaves.
It's my turn to investigate.

I use years of calculated
boyish recklessness
to hoist myself over the wall
onto the inner ledge,
much to her horror,
and can barely make out
crosses in the dusk
when she coaxes my
frame back on the side
of the living.

It's Sunday.
The Old Cemetery's closed.
Even the dead need a day off
from the nosy living.

The graves, they say, date
back to the 1800s.
British colonisers, mostly.
Unable at last to unsettle
their unwilling hosts.

*The sins they must have committed
to have been buried in an alien land,
doomed for the rest of eternity
to look up at a god
they may have mocked while alive!*
She traces a trajectory in air,
her finger pointing to and fro
a temple and the graveyard
it overlooks.

Shiva, the destroyer of worlds,
sits proud in his monument
at the banks of the Ganga—
holy mother who
washes sins off the foulest
souls, they say.

See? How apt!
I show her
redemption
for the irredeemable.

Distance and daylight fail us.
We have a train to catch.
We'll never know
the epitaphs locked
beyond the gates,
much like the stories of
the many colonised
silenced to oblivion.

Justice?
I'm indecisive
for lack of information.

Previously published in *The Piker Press* (November 14, 2022)

Essential Services

My cousin, the know-it-all procrastinator,
would rather host *litti chokha* barbecues in his
backyard
than sit at the shop his father bleeds his pension for.

My uncle, tomorrow-man's father,
plays cards with his gang in the alley all day,
for there's no social distancing at the office.

The socially distanced animal's brother,
l'homme de la littérature,
has cancelled his gym membership
(one must not work out masked!)
and has long unmasked dinner chats
with the pretty lady down the street.

The immunity conscious pretty lady,
doctor's wife and too good for our town,
nibbles on *sushi* and stuffs her enamoured husband
with last night's leftover *seekh kebabs.*

The French *littérateur's* woman,
president of Gossipers Anonymous,

holds the weight-watcher's witch trials at her place
to avoid evening rush at the vegetable market.

The diabetic doctor, husband of the alleged witch,
sermons at-risk gluttons on weekdays
and on weekends attacks the crowded corner bakery
armed with insulin jabs.

The baker's wife who'd rather keep
her twelve children out of school than risk infection,
crams them in the lorry headed for the market,
for she needs no less than
the baker's dozen to carry her ingredients.

The lorry driver who won't wear a mask for
how-on-earth-would-he-spit-*khaini*-in-one,
forbids his wife from visiting Gossipers Anonymous
hotspots.

The lorry driver's wife,
sulking at her overanxious tobacco-chewer,
vents out by inviting her aunts and sisters from across
town
for risk-free lunch at her home.

One of her sisters,
nurse and my mother's friend,
gladly accepts mother's invitation
to bring her kin over for dinner at our place.

My mother, furious at my precautionist father
who didn't take her out shopping

and went to play cards himself,
insists that I bring my band
for an acoustic set at the ladies' dinner.

I, fully aware that gatherings
must be avoided for the good of all,
am slipping out at dusk
to have my poem peer-reviewed
at my know-it-all cousin's barbecue.

litti chokha: a popular vegetarian dish from the Indian states of Bihar, Jharkhand, and Uttar Pradesh
l'homme de la littérature: French for "the man of literature"
sushi: a Japanese dish typically prepared with sticky rice and some type of fish or seafood, all rolled and steamed together
seekh kebab: a meat dish made by assembling spiced minced meat on skewers and cooking on a barbecue or a tandoor (clay oven)
littérateur: a person who is interested in and knowledgeable about literature
khaini: a type of smokeless tobacco made from cured tobacco leaves; khaini, mixed with choona (flaked lime), is placed between the lower lip and lower front teeth to allow nicotine absorption, and is spat thereafter
Previously published in *Roi Fainéant Press* (February 2022)

UDAY SHANKAR OJHA
Seeds

What is your vogue
is not my forte!
Heralds my own tribe
as he departs to board his plane.
His potato chips are too crispy
and the proud burger,
too disdainful, mocks
the soggy curry-soaked rice on
my poor banana leaf.

The fate of a few
customary pleasantries
hang in vain.

My father suffered,
practised the same burden,
feared I could plant my pollen
in an alien land.
Fear infects even
in cases of true credentials
carried carefully,
or seeds sown
in an accustomed earth.

Wish we sense it early
lest the vogue should suffer
a reshuffle.

Sacrament

It is at midnights
often
that exploration ceases.

Stuffed mortal beings,
to their utter surprise,
get nowhere
at the end of the search.

For centuries,
living on sand
ended only
in artful rhetoric.

Yet somewhere,
the wish to revive in us
the gods immortal
persists violently,

and you cannot curb
the blind fury of guns
let loose
from straightened domes,
silencing innocent cries
on anarchic altars.

Congruence

Somehow my pen comes
to rest on you, though I ask only
for a meaningful poem.

Echoes of your sweet thrashes
cool me thrice over,
your eyes, spying,
melt ice to the core.

This year was destined
not to yield the least.
Loud was the land,
sapless, insipid yet
rigid, not to be ripped apart.

Yet the air around me
breathes unsparingly,
fumes and fragrances
conspiring adhesive designs.

SHABINA NISHAT OMAR
I Ponder On Peace

In a life fraught with turmoil, I pause and contemplate:
What is peace?
Is it the calm within? Or the serene exterior?
Is it elusive or is it attainable?
Is it a chimera or is it a mirage?
Is it an intangible entity or a tangible reality?
I ponder upon the occurrence
Of kaleidoscopic transformations
Watching glorious promises transform into sullen falsehoods.
Understanding stolid forever transformed
Into shimmering transience
Realizing that peace glitters, subsides, ravages
And is mangled into convenience.
I ponder as I gaze on the vagaries of human optimism across
nations:
Efforts, promises, politics, compromises, negotiations…
Endless engagements.
I ponder on the shifting shapes of peace;
The unyielding quest of its attainment.
I ponder from within the depths of my mind.
I reflect standing on the observation deck of my soul.
I muse poised on the brink of every seismic heartbeat.
Only to be answered by resonating quietude:
Awaiting the tranquillity in life.

SWATI PAL
Stray Thoughts On Amity

Legs swinging
In unison
As we sat aloft
The branches
Of guava trees
In Lucknow Cantt,
No words uttered
Nor required,
Only the happy munching
Of unripe unwashed guavas
Relished together
By a bunch
Of starry-eyed kids
Waiting to fly
Into the endless sky.

Was that amity?

Apparel of a specific colour
Jackets or caps or stoles
Other paraphernalia
Of the many

Who walk and talk
And sit on *dharnas*
Or shout slogans
Or make promises
Or shed copious tears
Or speak fervently
Of global peace, brotherhood, emancipation,
Transparency, commitment, dedication
And and and…

Is this amity?

The sun moon and stars
Exist in the same firmament
Each unique
Each divine
Each pure
Each sacred

This is perfect amity.

Amity springs not
From the stinking cesspool
Of individual
Or collective
Insecurities.

Amity grows
In interlocked fingers
Of coupling
Between partners
Who bask
In their own

And the other's
Light.

The sceptic
And I
Assume,
True amity
Can only be—
A dream.

dharna: Hindi for "a strike" or "a peaceful demonstration"

Anita Panda
Soldiers Never Die

The brave one fought and how!
Undaunted until his last breath
Fighting the lethal, ominous enemy within
Masking the pain, nausea, fatigue, and blue, chipped nails
With a brave heart's smile!

He fought each battle with supreme positivity
From the icy Kargil heights to Siachen
From the beautiful, bloody woods of Kashmir
To the scorching deserts of Thar
He fought each battle valiantly

And within his frail body
Raged the invisible enemy
Devouring his cells and organs greedily
Spreading like a wild ravaging fire

He fought and how!
Each attack of the insidious foe
Baring its fangs in glee
Calm and strong, unfazed, and indefatigable!

Braving the painful rounds of chemo with a stoic smile
Bearing each needle piercing his frail body
An optimist and warrior to the core
He fought and how!

Until his last breath
Supine on the ventilator in the cold ICU
Limbs swollen, lesioned liver, lungs, and spleen
Breathless and with eyes glazed
But not without one last fierce fight

And then he departed
Draped in the tri-colour
Cremated with full military honours
And a glorious gun salute!

An officer, gentleman, and true soldier!
Immortal and forever eternal
He lives on in the stars, Earth, oceans, winds, and fire
He lives on in the memories and songs of yesteryears
In the hearts he touched with compassion

He lives on through his legacy of courage and valour
As gentle as he was strong!
Gone from this earthly realm now
Merging into the infinite cosmos
Becoming clouds so he can return, again and again
To the motherland

He lives on through his indomitable spirit
Rest in peace, beautiful soul!
     For soldiers never die

Previously published in *Living On* (curated by Swati Pal, Hawakal Publishers, August 2022)

DURGA PRASAD PANDA
My Assassin And I

My assassin
And I,

We look for each other
Everywhere.

Knife in hand,
He is on the prowl

Around the world
Baying for my warm blood.

I play truant, camouflage, devise
Ways to escape his hawk eyes.

Wear wigs, moustache;
Even *salwars* and padded bras.

My assassin and I,
We spent an entire lifetime

Playing hide-n-seek
Exhausted, one day, I looked within

Went deep down the spiralling
Staircase of my own being.

And found him sitting hunched
In the dark corner

Of my heart
With his blood shot eyes

Like an angry kid wearing a long face;
Sharpening his knife

On the hard stone
Of my sad, white bones.

salwar: a pair of light, loose, pleated trousers, usually tapering to a tight fit
around the ankles, worn by women from South Asia

NIKITA PARIK
Skyline Of A Prayer

Fazr azaan breaks
the sky into two.
The lit half is a prayer.

Its glowing mouth spreads
through my language
and settles in my chest.

Maybe God is
the singular breath
that floods you whole?

Someone exhales
a muted *ardas*
somewhere.

It rises to the ether
and becomes
the sun.

All faith
prerequisites
abandonment

So this prayer
abandons me
and becomes itself.

Fazr: Arabic for "dawn prayer"
azaan: the Muslim call to ritual prayer
ardas: a Sikh prayer performed before or after undertaking any significant task
Previously published in *My City Is A Murder Of Crows* (Hawakal Publishers, July 2022)

A Ghazal For The Art Of Free-Falling

A blue serenity has forested where a stillness blooms,
A cold fire now abounds where a stillness blooms.

I shut my eyes, a calmness sweeps me over,
Silence like a song sounds where a stillness blooms.

Existence is but one deep breath centred into self,
Purposeful breathing resounds where a stillness blooms.

This life is a droplet hanging on the eyelash of fate,
Forgiveness is profound where a stillness blooms.

Drown yourself in this river, Nikita, for
Being lost is being found where a stillness blooms.

Previously published in *My City Is A Murder Of Crows* (Hawakal Publishers, July 2022)

Swimming

This evening, my city
is an old man, bent forward
in *Maghrib's Namaz:*

waves of faith
keep it afloat.

Maghrib: Arabic for "sunset prayer"
Namaz: the ritual prayers prescribed by Islam to be observed five times
a day
Previously published in *My City Is A Murder Of Crows* (Hawakal
Publishers, July 2022)

SUCHITA PARIKH-MUNDUL
Countries

Countries are Cubist paintings
with anthems hanging from their tongues,
garbled and in need of re-framing.
When the canvas fades,
a wildfire of calm will spread
so planetary things can take over:
cliches like flower buds and evergreens
and cool ocean breezes. Not to mention
varieties of stars that will send
such embraces of light,
everything will feel like love.
It'll be as if the Earth cracked open
and out poured this sweet seed
of contemplation,
unravelling fraught tensions,
colouring the world afresh.

What Is A Border?

A border is a visceral taste of culture. Its length and breadth outline a land of identity. The cartographers involved in its origination must have been whimsical or drunk when they stretched a line over all kinds of terrain in that Impressionist style.

It should be noted that this mapped line serves as a marker, diving the areas on either side. It's an official line of demarcation.

Imagine a centipede with its numerous limbs crossing this threshold in a state that science fiction deems plausible, i.e., being both here and there, all at once, with hundreds of sole prints across the imaginary divider.

However, as with everything else, the border too has metastasised. But hark, Spiritus Mundi is here, finally, to exhume the world from its mistakes.

Political Speech

is full of historic syllables,
many of which are anchored
to the invisible sound
of violins. Familiar consonants
with the fullness of vowels
are always promising
to soften the edges of conflict.
Messages we've heard (and those
we never will) have been gathering
discreetly like footnotes,
filling eyes, touching lips
with deep lines.
Ah, rhetoric. Its parenthetical
smile must be liberated.

BARNALI RAY SHUKLA
Coordinates Unknown

Born in a village
stitched to maps
embroidered with
names that granny
spoke in a language
of salt that mended
her wrinkles to
laugh lines, her cheeks
washed clean by tears

of something like
happiness, that
memories don't
lie buried like sons
who fell to mines
in a land altered
by whims,

truce comes later
than greed
but my father
and the holy

ghost still watch
over us, over time,
waiting

for the day
when guns fall
silent, seek
poetry of arms,
embrace a future
not scarred by
                    bullets.

The Wait Is Over

This shadow called it quits
left the source of light
as it waits for a flight
to where the crack once was

it needs a change.

The shadow stays folded
in a pocket where light
once was, waiting to be
claimed but you
only see light first

it needs a voice.

The shadow is a sign,
light is near
still you call it dark,
for once if you could
lose your shadow to
time when light was
out in the dark

it needs a hand.

The shadow is a note,
don't be too hard on
yourself, no need to
just twin with light
burning bright, burning

it needs a thought.

To make peace that
even dark
                    is bright.

Learning To Fly

The butterfly doesn't turn back
to the chrysalis that kept it safe
it has grown wings, seeks flight
lives on nectar and songs

Sometimes coloured
by notes of a ballad
held by the lens for a moment
fleeting or paused in time
for this one who lives for a day

A dance with flowers
beyond a winter of silence,
gently, for I haven't kept
time for it will go in time
paused only by the lines
you write in your song

before it stops breathing
not before it has showed
you gardens of wonder
held between the pages
of your dreams, even if

it's just for a day, flight
just for a day, colour
just for a day. I feared
the fragile till I met
a butterfly.

Tejaswinee Roychowdhury
Prophesy

One day, a tree will wear barbed wire for a crown
because a little boy will have tossed a seed
into the land between nations.

One day, roots will puncture marbled parliaments,
and legislative halls will be home
to a pair of Bengal tigers.

One day, bridges will be grape vines,
and tombs—rose bushes.

One day, certificates will be repurposed to pen love letters,
and paper currency shredded to confetti.

One day, we will learn there is no chaos in wilderness,
but emancipation in letting go.

One day, we will dance till dusk and dine at dawn,
and gaze at galaxies with a friend or a parent
or a cat invested in fireflies.

One day, we will forgive and mother each other;
step outside chalk circles and put a toe, a foot, in another
to see what the world looks like to a neighbour.

One day, gun barrels will hold lotuses,
and dismantled grenades will be wind chimes.

One day, constellations will mimic a human kiss,
and we will all be shooting stars rebuilding the universe.

This day will be born of choices—
yours and mine.

Symphony

All it took was a minute—

for your muscles to pin me to the apple tree
behind which we'd run to hide;

for the autumn sun to be your halo
when you arrested my eyes in yours;

for you to squeeze your thumb against my lips,
sneak a kiss on my ticklish collarbone;

for the orchard boy to follow us,
convinced we were stealing apples;

for you to assure him we weren't
while I hid my face behind your shoulder;

for us to coil our little fingers like twine,
smile at the oblivious tourists we'd left behind.

I've struck a bargain with the laws of the universe,
plucked that minute out of the space-time continuum;

because that minute is a symphony—
an addition to my collection of symphonies

where I seek tranquillity amidst storms.

MANISHA SAHOO
In The Company Of Quiet Solitude

When the trills get louder, more insistent,
so does the voice beckoning me away from
the luminous screen screaming of terror,
and strife, swords of words and otherwise;
bangles match the birdcall as her hands gesture
the urgency embodied by her summoning, and so
I go, a scathed heart in tow, to the balcony beyond—

Stillness, solitude descend upon us
while we search the green for red curved beaks,
a camouflaging pair of *sua*; bright blue glimpses
of a *neelakantha* until throaty calls divert us
towards a hopping *kumbhatua*; but my breath hitches
when I espy at last the playful leaps of yellow
and black, *haladi basanta*—mother's beloved.

The golden oriole finds its mate, the greater coucal
disappears amongst bushes, the Indian roller flies away,
and the parrots hide; we linger to the fading sounds,
I listen to the stories of her childhood long past,
her eyes lit up from memories beyond my grasp,
yet they embrace me, a shawl woven of fragments
of time and her voice, on a late spring afternoon.

sua: Odia for "parrot"
neelakantha: Odia for "Indian roller"
kumbhatua: Odia for "greater coucal"
haladi basanta: Odia for "Indian golden oriole"

SHRUTI SAREEN
Cocooned

You lie enclosed in your cocoon
And I sleep oblivious in mine.
Neighbours,
We live as strangers.
Only the whispering wind brushes
Us together, and we touch, at times.
Stray insects that crawl over you
Crawl over me too.
When the cocoons burst, will we
Recognise, will we realise
That we are sisters born
Of the same butterfly?

Previously published in *Aainanagar* (August 14, 2016)

MINAL SAROSH
Senryu Poems

(1)
refugee
his heart beats
in two countries

(2)
unmarked grave
a dog sitting quietly
near the mound

(3)
world peace
a ferris wheel going
round and round

SHOBHA SENGUPTA
Alone

She sat alone with her thoughts.
This lockdown has been good to her.
She is rested, restored, rejuvenated.

She can plan her itineraries in peace.
The world is small and yet too large to traverse for a non traveller.

A sedentary person,
Her waking hours consumed by the written word of others.
Unable to express herself,

Pulls and pushes of different types,
Of different worlds,
Clash and smash against her bones
Like waves of the sea.

While tidal waves, even storms crash over her,
She is seemingly impervious. For someone said:
It doesn't matter what others do to you.
It matters what you do to yourself.

Therapy is a word she examines carefully.
Who needs it,
When she has friends who read the
books she sells?

SANJEEV SETHI
Plea For Peace

Urgency is an attitude. The lever to check it lies
within us. Unthinkingly we cross wayposts until
hindsight lobs its handbook at us.

The sour notes of dissonance must be sidelined
in the waste basket of history with the sincerity
and stamina they deserve.

If we attend to peace and its attendant virtues as
casually as another nosh with our nightly sips:
our kids will never be able to enjoy their apéritifs.

Wagah

Boughs
of the same cedar
now apart
disinterested
in each other
like a couple
now divorced.

Wagah
you expunge fellow feelings
and herald
hymns of hate.

Wagah: A border town straddling the line between India and Pakistan
Previously published in *Suddenly For Someone* (Atma Ram & Sons, Delhi,
1988)

Warfare

Ugliness raises its banner on the globe. You and I
sight images exhibiting the hecatombs of hostilities
activated by hubris and hauteur.

The air I inhale blends with the soot of spoliation.
Funk and fear buff my lanes. The specter of cruor
and carnage stalk the sensations.

ONCE I PUTIN, I DON'T PULL OUT: memes
frequent the inbox. Twitter is where apprehensions
are exchanged with aliens and acquaintances.

But it can be harnessed to hatch pro-peace atmospherics.
The gateway to a glorious future requires pacifism as its
password: beatific inferences boost peacefulness.

SHANTA SHARAN
Tales Told

Tales untold of
Tall men
Fell into my ears
In passing

My mother
Invited to
Encourage
The half listening
Ears
Of my fidgety
School
Spoke

Softly said
I was five
Or six
Or maybe seven
Years old
Like many others
In Wardha
I had a special bond
With Bapu

Before a *padyatra*
On a sun-tired day
We trooped to Bapu
Armed with our question
What is our task
Today, Bapu?
A kind smile
Sized up
The eager
Battalion

Run ahead
Little children
Remove stones
Pick thorns
Toss the rubbish
From the path
That your elders
Tread upon
Make their journey easy
Let their stride flow

Happily, we skipped
Clearing the
Stubborn stones
Spiky thorns
Rough rocks
That were carelessly strewn
On the walking path

The task that day
Was one of many lessons
Learnt for life

My mother stopped
Speaking
The children
Continued to listen

Wardha: Mahatma Gandhi's residence from 1936 to his demise in 1948
Bapu: a Gujarati endearment for "father"; the title given to Mahatma Gandhi by Subhas Chandra Bose in 1944
padyatra: a march or pilgrimage on foot

Marigolds In An Urn

Plucked heads bob gallantly
Russet red ochre gold and tangerine
In the brass urn decorating the space
Uncomplaining
In their dance of death
Before the final dump
Unmindful
Of the few
That pay scant heed
To the silent passage
From one life to another

Why Despair?

Nudge the switch inside of you
A white glow you will birth
Snuffing worms
Doubts of imagination
Querulous, tenacious
Nibbling your insides

A hidden gourmet
Of your sterling
Worth will surface
Filling your plate
With the delectable fare
Of the rich coded recipe
Drawn from the cells that carouse
And give you
Your inimitable mark

ANEETA SHARMA
If The World Were My Canvas

What colour would I pick—
A riot of rainbow hues?
Crimson of blood let free
Or blue from the deep sea
Green? The way we want it to be?

The saffron of valour
bright yellow of mustard fields
purple borrowed from royalty
Or red from the flames of fire
Earthy brown or playful pink
...?

I think I may favour black
for I know it will include
tenaciously trap and hold
Every single variant shade
within its generous fold

Or perhaps the purity of white
will be a better bet
with it I can rejoice

in the sheer absence
of unmitigated choice

Yes, definitely white
Which favours nought
fresh, indivisible white
of daisies, clouds and fleece
of simplicity, innocence and peace

Peace Is A Fickle Bird

Peace is a fickle bird
poised on a precarious perch
It clutches with eager claws
a rickety, tottering bar
that tilts every now and again
impaled on a fulcrum of power.

She exists in easy equilibrium,
her tiny heart quelling
before shades of dissension
Keen eye fixed on wobbly scales
she flits away on flighty wings
the minute the balance sways.

Let us then establish equations
which are not steeped in crimson
Rise before it is too late
and rest our games of power
Let us build a house of equality
that she may inhabit now and forever.

BRIT SHNEUER
The Reservation

A walk I will not take
in the Reservation when the night—thick black—
curtain drops down
and for once a day, becomes unreserved

The invisible Nature Spirits
rolling in purple thorns, erase the walking path
for snakes and gazelles to pass
bringing back the fireflies
Families of boars come out of their hiding bush to
graze
on freshly dug roots and sweet cactus fruits
Silver rippling off the mongoose backs
glitter-vanish-glitter play in the coloured black air
Foxes invite their mates
to eat wild grapes, dig and bury and tussle in the sand
Howling jackals igniting each other to an orchestra of
complaints
Leaves sipping dew crystals between the day's dusty grains
Goats' hairy milky smell linger among trees
On rocks and boulders still sunny hot, geckos sprawl

Do spiders sleep?

Trees communicating wordlessly, innocent vulnerable filigrees
Granting an amnesty to us all

My night is thick with inherited un-humanness
Afraid of the suffering this world can inflict

Retreat as the living entity of the trees
Nevertheless come round to germinate

SONYA SINGH VERMA
Keep The Peace

My sister/our sister
Is now
Confined
In a psychiatric ward
For the last one year
When she gets angry
And threatens
To break TV sets and smash people's faces
They run for cover
And reminisce in bewildered whispers
About
My sister
The "gold medallist"
Married off at 23 to a "good boy"
Same caste, secure job, there was love…
And then
The beatings began
And the coverups
Learn how to bear up
This happens in every home
Keep the peace

She tried to *keep the peace*
He bludgeoned her with words
Hails of hurtful abuse
He bludgeoned her
With demands
He bludgeoned her
With commands
Do not speak, question, or answer back
He bludgeoned her
With harangues
Why can't you be like so and so's
Wife,
Mother,
Daughter,
Daughter-in-law?

Battered, tired, defeated
She kept the peace
And one day, the dam cracked
Burst
Almost drowning
Sputtering, gagging
She emerged
Enraged
Violent,
Incoherent

Whenever her old self would remember to *keep the peace*
She would stare vacantly
Out of the hospital window
Or sob inconsolably
Into her pillow
Keep the peace, they said

The Thing With Peace Is—

It's so tenuous
Fragile
Temporary
Delusional

Its surface calm
Is rippled so easily
With a pebble
All it takes is just one pebble

Just one person
Can shatter the mirage
The invader
Who pounces on land that was always *his*
The guerrilla fighting an *unjust* war
The terrorist proselytising *faith*
The keeper of *morals*
Whipping up *holy* diktats
Of submission
A fundamentalist spewing indignation

All it takes is just one person

How Do Those Women Speak?

They sit huddled and fearful
Cloistered in barren, bombed landscapes
Shrouded in swathes of claustrophobia
Diminished
Forbidden to think
Forged in precast conscripted roles
Forbidden to walk alone
Sold to known old men
Raw unspeakable cruelties
They can never ever expunge
From their bodies, minds, and souls

How do these women speak?
I hear they form secret sororities
And speak in swiftly changing codes
Behind heavily barricaded doors
Their collective rage
Smothered in impotent inability
To move, do, act, breathe

What if they self-immolate?
And raze the earth
Their collective fires

Scorching all child-bearing wombs
Maybe the future will not bear
The monsters who shackled their tongues
Rising from their ashes
My God,

I hope those women will be able to speak one day
Freely, fluidly, fearlessly

Indra Somaiah
He Too Was Like Me

I went to his house and saw
He too had a mother
She too was weeping

Do not ask about the state of his wife
And the daughter, so little

His life was taken by my hand
And mine by his

I went to his house and saw
He too was like me

PRAMOD SUBBARAMAN
Mahsa

In her name, they fought and died
Iranians, fought and died

Her killing was the last straw
Brave girls and boys, fought and died

The promise was never kept
Every day, they fought and died

This time, we hope that they win
The heroes, they fought and died

Pramod salutes those brave souls
For freedom, they fought and died

Revolting

Join the Bhakt revolution, my friend
Bring glory to our country again
Forget the past, this is the latest trend

They have failed to atone, to make amends
Now we will show them the meaning of pain
Join the Bhakt revolution, my friend

I find it difficult to comprehend
When did my neighbour become a villain?
Forget the past, this is the latest trend

This time, no compromise, we will not bend
We will continue until they are slain
Join the Bhakt revolution, my friend

But they are my friends too, I must defend
Aju, Javed, Murtuza, and Hussain
Forget the past, this is the latest trend

Stop the war! Share in the peace dividend
End the segregation, be one again
Join the Bhakt revolution, my friend
Forget the past, this is the latest trend

Which Road Should We Take?

It is that time again
To think about options
Which path lessens the pain?
I hate these decisions

To think about options
In this time of crisis
I hate these decisions
No God here to help us

In this time of crisis
Twenties' Thirties' full fury
No God here to help us
Which is this century?

Twenties' Thirties' full fury
Thought it was in the past
Which is this century?
Did not think it would last

Thought it was in the past
They even told us so
Did not think it would last
Painful to see them go

They even told us so
We were fed with those lies
Painful to see them go
Watch as another dies

We were fed with those lies
For this country we bled
Watch as another dies
Rivers of blood, he said

For this country, we bled
In so much fear, we shake
Rivers of blood, he said
That blood, is in a lake

For my family's sake
It is that time again
Which road should we take?
Which path lessens the pain?

Previously published in *Green Ink Poetry* (September 02, 2020)

MARION VERWEIJ
Space For Peace

Peace is longed for by all,
        but we drive it constantly away,
Yet give it the opportunity,
        and it would gladly stay.
So where then to begin
        in giving it a safe space?
What is attractive to peace,
        what emplacement and pace?
Peace has retreated to the forest,
        to the lake and the mountain,
What the ecology attractive to
        its free-flowing, healing fountain?

Peace is always there close by,
        as we continually call its name,
But there needs to be an inner quiet,
        so it can feel a same same.
Peace is where I can be found,
        and yet where I am not.
It is in being with the better me,
        the inner noise forgot.
Peace creates a quiet confidence

that upholds and is intact,
It looks at the bigger picture
not only the singular fact

Peace perpetuates patience
and is found in tranquil places.
It is timeless, enduring and still,
and has many faces.
To look oneself in the mirror
reflecting you did your best to be right,
Brings the peace of mind of being clean,
of bringing a bit more light.
If the human has but a humility
to ensure the ego call cease,
We will find that where it resides
there is no space for lack of peace.

Us And Them

In response to a conference on extreme violence in the world

We're better than you because we're strong.
We're stronger than you because we're weak.
We're oppressed by you because we are poor.
We despise you because you don't understand.
We were born in this location therefore share the true belief.
We hold secrets you don't and that gives us power.
We have in abundance so feel good to give to those with less.
We carry our badge of guilt that separates us from you.
We understand the real truth and patronise those who don't.
We are excluded and must fight to show our worth.
We are we.
You are you.
And never the twain shall meet.

I want to belong, to feel less lost, to find a home.
I want to be confirmed for who and what I am.
I want to be recognised for all my glory.
I want to be less afraid, unsure and insignificant.

I want to be understood, received and valued.
I want to walk tall, feel proud, radiate dignity.
I want to be loved, to be cherished, just for being me.
I want to not have a fear of stillness, of being with me alone.
I want to escape all this pain and misery.
I want to know I go somewhere better when I die.
I am alone.
You are alone.
But we cannot reach each other.

Is my heart better than my head?
My kidney more important than my spleen?
Should I be a feeler or a thinker as a way of life?
Should I ignore my spirit in favour of my brain?
Can I feel united with my many lives?
Can I give each a chance to be at best?
Can I set the different inner places in me free?
Can I find the inner stillness no one can remove me from?
Can I dare go within, find the home in me,
The place of inner belonging?
Can I feel the Creator in me, the universe in me,
A part of the greater whole?
If so then I am not I.
You are not you.
Together we belong as one kind.

Previously published in *Touching Tomorrow* by Marion Verweij and Mark Stolk (June 2020)

ELIANE VIGNERON
And Then

And then—
my *heart* smiles
All my cells
sparkling, this emotion is as the laugh
of a baby conversing with angels around her
Crystalline
as water droplets from a river
skipping from stone to stone
on a fresh bright winter morning

And then—
my *mind* recognises
and ackowledges
that sensation, that *emotion*
of all of *me*
connected to the entire *god-universe*,
wholly whole and protected,
as when *heart* and *mind* are in *joy*
    jointly
        my *soul* sighs, tranquil. I am at *peace*.

And then—
my *peace* glows, pulsing
from inside, all benefit from it.
Being a channel of glowing calm, each
of us radiating, creating that
ripple effect,
growing together like waves
of tranquility from where everything
is possible, for our highest good.
Gratitude to become that magic wand,
that incandescent tube, for all to enjoy
        in joy
peace of mind
peace of heart
peace of soul

And then—my *heart* smiles

"Recognize that peace is the wholeness created by right relationships with oneself, other persons, other cultures, other life, Earth, and the larger whole of which all are a part." ~ *The Earth Charter*

ACKNOWLEDGEMENTS

My sincerest gratitude to H.E. Ouided Bouchamaoui, Nobel Peace Prize laureate 2015, and Padma Shri Agus Indra Udayana, Founder—Ashram Gandhi Puri, Bali, for adding their voices to *Amity*.

I am indebted to Shri Naveen Patnaik, Hon'ble Chief Minister of Odisha, for his words of encouragement.

I thank Dr. Harbeen Arora Rai, Founder & President—G100, Bitan Chakraborty, Founder—Hawakal, and Kiriti Sengupta, Chief Editor—*Ethos Literary Journal*, for endorsing the idea of this book. Thanks, also, to Kiriti *Da* for suggesting its title and to Bitan for designing the cover.

Many thanks to Amrit Kiran Singh, Humra Quraishi, Maheekshita Mishra, Mary Denniz, Nazma Naheed, Rao Gulshan, and Vijayant Thapa for their steadfast support.

To Reeham and Shakil Ahmed, my unending love.

Lightning Source UK Ltd.
Milton Keynes UK
UKHW012359231222
414383UK00006B/403